TAKE HEED

A Time of Persecution-Vol. 4

Take Heed, Vol. 4
A Time of Persecution
Copyright © 2022 by Austin Campo

Additional copies may be ordered from the publisher for educational,
business, promotional or premium use.
For information, contact ALIVE Book Publishing at:
alivebookpublishing.com, or call (925) 837-7303.

Book Cover and Interior design by Alex P. Johnson

ISBN 13
978-1-63132-161-0

Library of Congress Cataloging-in-Publication Data
is available upon request.

First Edition

Published in the United States of America by ALIVE Book Publishing
and ALIVE Publishing Group, imprints of Advanced Publishing LLC
3200 A Danville Blvd., Suite 204, Alamo, California 94507
alivebookpublishing.com

PRINTED IN THE UNITED STATES OF AMERICA

10 9 8 7 6 5 4 3 2 1

TAKE HEED

A Time of Persecution-Vol. 4

Austin Campo

ABOOKS

Alive Book Publishing

FOREWORD

Merriam Webster, at https://www.merriam-webster.com/ dictionary/persecution, says that persecution is: "the act or practice of persecuting especially those who differ in origin, religion, or social outlook." It is simplified but does say the general meaning clearly and concisely.

Dictionary.com's 3rd definition, found at: https://www.dictionary.com/browse/persecution describes it as: "a program or campaign to exterminate, drive away, or subjugate people based on their membership in a religious, ethnic, social, or racial group." Notice that they mention a plan to *exterminate*.

Worldwide we have witnessed people hating other people based on race. In many places of the world people have witnessed different religious beliefs or sects of beliefs being at the crux of division and warring. Even as of late, we have all been party to strong and loud divides for political reasons, each believing their side is the only way. Even wearing a mask or getting a vaccine has continued chiseling a chasm that has always existed since sin entered the world God created.

Some people have no opinions while others have many. The world though, is moving faster and closer to completely turning away from its Creator. As this happens, persecution will grow *worldwide*. Christian beliefs and the actions or inactions of believers will be categorized as intolerant, insolent and terroristic when they try to defend themselves. Worldwide, believers will be sought, imprisoned, or killed. It will not be only certain countries carrying out these actions.

In Luke 14:28, Jesus posed a question: "*For which of you, desiring to build a tower, does not first sit down and count the cost, whether he has enough to complete it?*" This is what it feels. He is asking now. Have we considered it all? Are we ready? Have we truly counted the costs? Persecution *is* coming. Count the cost. God bless and *take heed!*

CHAPTER ONE

The Beginning of the End

Every volume of the series I start, I always go to God with questions. This would not surprise my husband, because I am a "question girl." Somehow, it's just the way I think and process. I never outgrew being inquisitive. This is the one set of questions I am usually answered quickly.

I always ask what the name of the book is. However, this time I didn't have to ask because the ministering angels told me before volume 3 was even finished. That, however, has not been the norm'.

I ask how many chapters it will have. I ask what God dreams or visions He wants in the book I am on. I ask what He wants the Foreword to be about, and I always either ask what the chapter name is or what the chapter is about.

In this case, I just remembered to ask yesterday. This book should have six chapters. The Foreword was to be generally about persecution and that it's coming, check, check!

Then this chapter name came, with a ministering angel spelling it out, "The Beginning of the End." Repeating the title aloud, it reminded me that I was already told that at least one of the dreams or visions in this book is during the tribulation period. As for the others, I haven't been given whether they are in the time leading up to or during. The chapter name here, though, seems ominous.

Moving forward, if you've read any of the other volumes, you know I number the dreams or visions He *specifically* says will be in it, before the book starts. He then usually adds others, but I don't number those. Lastly, if I write like I'm talking to you, it's because I am. With that's, let's continue!

#1 The Book Lost
Received: April 11, 2014

Before I relay the dream, I will explain why this is called the "book lost." The Lord gave me a dream that was like looking at anything while awake. It was clear and in color. While having it I could *hear, see,* and *feel* everything going on. Yet when I woke up it seemed I visually could only still *see* part but *knew* much more. Somehow though, at the time, I still ignorantly let it all go.

A little time went on and the pieces and parts started coming back through, flittering through my mind. I would be on task doing something else, and there would come a thought, then another. I knew He was not letting me just let this one go. So, I asked Him about it and I prayed about it. Somewhere into this process, the ministering angels reminded me that years before He said I would write a book, "at least" one. The moment that thought hit my spirit, I *knew,* He was writing a book from what I saw! At the time that's about all I knew. I did not know it was prophecy for sure, though I wondered that a little. I decided that since I wasn't sure, it would at least be a very interesting Christian surmising or adventure story. So, I proceeded to write.

To be honest, I wasn't sure how to go about it. I was not relaxed and just relaying. I thought everything had to be better, better than how my thoughts roll out or I could explain. So, it was a very slow process. Then, part-way in, the computer's motherboard died, and I had no back-up at the time. It wasn't very good thinking ahead on my part, but alas, the truth. So, God wanted a book on what is relayed in this dream clear back in 2014. Therefore, I am calling it "The Book Lost."

The Dream

My husband and I were in our house. We were moving toward the door. Our voices were kind-of muted, until he said, "It's about time." In the dream, *I knew* it was almost 7:00 p.m.

We walked out onto the porch and sat down on the hammock-type swings we have there. *I felt* pensive. We were talking but our words were obscured until I heard my husband say "It'll be hard to keep the animals soon. They'll take them for food."

We heard vehicles coming down the road from the west, and we stood up and stepped closer to the front of our porch. Just then, I saw a small motorcade of four extremely shiny, extremely black vehicles passing slowly. It was one large, oddly tall truck with three SUVs following. They seemed to almost pause as they drove slowly beyond the tree line, to the clear part. Then they continued passing and went up the hill east of us. *I felt* relieved.

He and I were walking back into the house, and I said aloud, "It's still sad what it's come to here." *I knew* it was that way because of something President Obama instructed. Then the dream switched.

It was daytime, bright and sunshiny. It, again, was like

I was seeing out of my eyes. I was outside on the porch, and I saw a Sheriff pull in and get out of his car. I waved. He was smiling and hollered up toward my husband. He did not come up the hill of our drive. He stayed down on the turn-around we have.

I watched as my husband walked down. *I felt* a lot of anxiety, and I watched in silence. I saw from where I was that they were having a conversation. I saw my husband turn, and he was smiling as he was talking, but I knew it was feigned. It was not like when he is relaxed. *I felt* more nervous.

I then saw the Sheriff kind-of nod, and his countenance looked a little different than the welcoming face he had when he got out of his vehicle. They said their good-byes, then my husband walked back up the drive as the Sheriff left.

Before he even got to me, I asked if everything was okay. I seemed to be down off the porch in the high part of the drive by then. He looked at me and said something under his breath that made me not say anything else. There was a tenseness. As he passed by me though, He said, "He tried to get me to say yes. I think he might suspect." Then the dream switched again.

The last part was brief. It was daytime, and very overcast. He and I were out by the drive near a telephone pole that has a security light on it, but the light was off.

I knew he was heading out and I felt really concerned about him going. He was holding something that looked like an architectural plan or scroll rolled up. I tried to explain that it was more dangerous than before, but he just said, "Pray, and I'll be back by 6:00." Then he started heading northeast off our acreage. This was the end of the dream.

I knew some of the dream immediately. I gained some more interpretation sometime soon after. Then I was given a lot more information when God took me back to it, and I started to write the original book, and a little as I started this one.

Interpretation

Part 1: Martial law will be imposed. We are ordered home, or to be at home, by a certain time. They will have ways to make sure this is enforced, and they will check *every day*. This will be instituted due to a law that went into effect when President Obama was in office.

I had no idea what exactly this meant, as I do not know everything that he, or any President, put into action. Just this last week, on a quick getaway with my husband, I read my friend Becky what I had so far. Just after, I felt led to try to find what President Obama might have signed that would be connected. So, I did.

What I found was that President Obama signed the NDAA (National Defense Authorization Act), which authorizes the *indefinite military detention* of persons the government suspects of involvement in terrorism, including U.S. citizens on U.S. soil. Prior, President George W. Bush signed the AUMF (Authorization of Use of Force) in 2001, which also gave the military ability to use necessary force to apprehend anyone having anything to do with the 9/11 attacks and anyone aiding or abetting anyone that did. However, the NDAA made more pointed provisions for the military to exercise their authority to do so.

When this happens, it will be instituted or approved and paid for by the Representatives and Senators on

Capitol Hill, as in the dream, the black motorcade was going *east, up the hill.*

Our time to be seen at home was approximately 7:00, so initial orders will be curfew at 7:00 p.m.

The situation was serious, and we knew disobeying would result in a very bad outcome.

Animals being taken for food means food is scarce. There will be shortages, and access to food will be limited or very low. It likely also is literal, meaning that the authorities or other people will take what you have, even your animals, to eat.

I commented that it was sad what it had come to this, "here," meaning in the United States.

Part 2: Sheriffs will be *the* authority in the counties (or parishes if this is nationwide). *I was given* this. *I* also *felt* that police departments had been disbanded. Whatever is taking place at the time, the number of authority figures in each county is down. Therefore, the Sheriffs will try to recruit those that are able to use a firearm and that are or *seem to be adhering* to the new way of life. In the dream, he was trying, again, to recruit my husband. Some people will appear to be going along with things on the surface, trying to get by as long as they can. There will be consequences when you are found not to be.

I feel this part also will include the NDAA actively taking place. Though I saw the Sheriff, who was trying to recruit my husband, rather than the military, *the feeling* was that there were dire circumstances for not being compliant with the new rules, whatever they were.

Part 3: It was overcast because times are getting darker by then. We were near the security light pole but the light was off, to show there will be no electric and we will have no security.

My husband leaving with the scroll or architectural plans in his hand was because there will be networks of people that will be helping each other, but it is all off grid. I was told, there would be *drops* where people leave maps, information updates gathered, and supplies.

He told me to pray, and he'd be back by 6:00 because it was a reminder that there was still a curfew to keep and most importantly, **to have faith in God.**

CHAPTER TWO

What Was Will Be Again

The title speaks of the persecution of the Christian church. The ministering angels relayed the name of this chapter's title. They can because they have the finished books of this series. I asked aloud because I was at a loss as I sat here, trying to figure out what I needed to relay next. Maybe it would have been more fitting to say "What Was Is, and Will Escalate," because the truth is, persecution has happened all along. It is happening now in other parts of the world. It will happen worldwide in the not so distant future.

Let me state that persecution can certainly happen for more than a belief in God or the following of Christ. However, this book will concentrate on the persecution of the Christians and other dissenters as the end time, or "end of all time" as we know it, comes closer.

However, before we move forward, let's take look back. Even before Jesus's death and resurrection, believers were persecuted for their faith.

Jeremiah was a prophet who has often been called, "the weeping prophet." Some have also saw Jeremiah a bit symbolic of Jesus Himself, not as a weeping prophet but on many other counts, perhaps mostly due to suffering for the sake of carrying out his call.

He was also a captive prophet. He was upset about the hardships he faced, and he brought it to God, who basically said he would suffer even more.

He was beaten and locked in stocks. He was mocked and belittled. The people he tried to warn called him a false prophet, accusing him of lying. At one point a death sentence was handed down to him, all because he chose to say yes to God. Ultimately, though not in the bible, other sources surmise he was stoned to death, per tradition, by his own people. These were the ones he'd tried to warn. Remember, this was pre-Jesus on the scene. Despite it all though, he was faithful.

Shadrach, Meshach, and *Abednego* were thrown into a fiery furnace because King Nebuchadnezzar commanded that any time various instruments were played, everyone would fall and worship the golden image he made, but these three would not.

The King was furious and had his guards heat up the furnace seven times hotter than normal. Still, Shadrach, Meshach and Abednego stood their ground. They knew there was only one God, and they would not worship another. Boldly, they answered back that they would not worship other gods or the image that the King had made.

Unlike so many that suffered persecution, these three were saved from death, *miraculously*. Though the furnace was so hot it killed the guards just by throwing the three in, the three young men were seen walking around, inside the fire. What's more, a fourth man was seen by the King! I think we can guess the Who that might be by now!

When the door was opened, the three came out to the King's amazement, and not a hair or piece of clothing was singed, and they did not smell like smoke. The King blessed their God, *testified* of how the three would not worship any other god but their own, and how they came out alive, even unharmed. He made a decree that that no one of any nation, who spoke any language could ever say anything against Shadrach, Meshach, and Abednego's God, or they would be cut to pieces and their houses would be destroyed. He said no other God could deliver the way he'd witnessed. You can read this story in Daniel Chapter 3, any bible version.

Daniel, was thrown into the lion's den because did not listen to the King's order which said for three weeks everyone must only give honor or worship to Darius the King Himself. In other words, no one could worship any other god. However, Daniel continued to pray to *the* God.

As it had been made a decree, those who hated Daniel and were jealous of the King's fondness of him, made a point to question the King about what must happen to anyone that did not obey the order. Punishment was to be thrown to the lions. Then they presented the King with the fact Daniel had broken the law. Though the King was upset about Daniel facing sure death, he did have him taken and thrown in.

Afterward, the king went back and fasted and was unable to sleep. In the morning he went to the lion's den and called out to Daniel, who answered. The astonished King quickly had him removed from the den, and listened as Daniel explained that God had shut the lions' mouths and they did not hurt him.

The King did two things after witnessing the unexpected. To paraphrase, He had Daniel's accusers and their families thrown into the lions' den, where they were violently killed. He also made a new decree that everyone from everywhere must tremble and fear Daniel's God, for He surely *is* the God who delivers, even from the lions' den.

However, as stated before, people are not always given a miraculous end. Sometimes the persecution is ongoing for long periods, causing physical and mental harm, and instantly or eventually for many, even death.

Mary, mother of Jesus, was betrothed to a carpenter named *Joseph* when she became pregnant, by supernatural means. This was part of God's plan. Though there is not much in the bible written about her plight, as far as *persecution* on that count, it would appear she was sent to an older cousin's house sometime during her pregnancy. Later, Mary and Joseph, had to leave everything and flee to Egypt, as an angel came to Joseph in a dream, warning him to *flee* to avoid King Herod's decree to kill all the male children two years and under.

Stephen was appointed by the Apostles to serve the Hellenists. He lived in Jerusalem. Some versions call him a deacon. Whatever name, he was not an Apostle, but a believer who was set into servant leadership. He served them, helping them to further understand living out a life as a believer, and he talked and preached. Most accounts say he was gifted in evangelizing, i.e., presenting the belief and seeing people come to accept Jesus as the risen Son of God.

He was falsely accused of speaking blasphemies against Moses and God Himself. Ultimately, his belief and commitment got him thrown out of town and stoned to death, *literally*. This means an angry mob picked up rocks, small and large, and hurled them at him, until he died. His miracle came *in his dying*, as he stated aloud that he saw the "Son of Man," Jesus, in the clouds, standing to the right of Father God. Then he died. So as his last selfless act, *he testified*. His story can be found in: Acts: 7, any bible version.

He is also often credited as the first Christian *martyr*, simply meaning, the first one to die for the cause of Christ, after Christ was risen.

Peter, also called Simon Peter, was one of the first to say yes to Jesus, jumping up out of his fishing boat with his brother Andrew when Jesus said, *"Come. Follow me, and I will make you fishers of men."* Matt. 4:19. He also got to walk on the water, like Jesus, until his faith waned. Jesus even called him the Rock, on which He would build His church, because before being told, Peter knew Jesus was the Christ, so Christ knew he could only know that by Father God.

Just like all of us, Peter also had weaknesses. He was impetuous, and likely had some anger issues to work through. When Jesus prepared to be taken to his ultimate death, Peter said it would not happen. Jesus rebuked him, saying, "Get behind me satan!" At the last supper, Jesus told Peter before the day ended, Peter would deny Him three times. It is assumed that he probably thought, "No, not me." However, he did. You can find this in the bible in Matthew 26:34. Then, when the soldiers came to arrest Jesus, Peter lashed out and cut off one of the soldier's ears!

Peter was not without persecution though. He was beaten, accused, and incarcerated several times by the religious leaders of the time.

In the end, he was crucified. This is probably the most known death for the cause, outside of Jesus Himself. Why? Peter felt he did not deserve to be crucified in the same manner of his Lord. Therefore, he requested that he be crucified upside down. They obliged.

Paul, previously Saul of Tarsus, was Jewish by descent. "A Pharisee of Pharisees," by his own description. He took well to the Roman agenda to persecute the followers of *"the Way"*. He was a great soldier for them, aggressive, determined, and cruel.

Later, after his conversion, he testified: *"I persecuted the followers of this Way to their death, arresting both men and women and throwing them into prison."* Acts 22:4 NKJV

The Jewish people and other prominent people of society who were not of the Way, sought to put him to death. Paul, speaking in II Corinthians 11:22-28 NKJV says: *"Are they Hebrews? So am I. Are they Israelites? So am I. Are they the seed of Abraham? So am Are they ministers of Christ? I speak as a fool. I am more: in labors more abundant, in stripes above measure, in prisons more frequently, in deaths often. From the Jews five times I received forty stripes minus one. Three times I was beaten with rods; once I was stoned; three times I was shipwrecked; a night and a day I have been in the deep; in journeys often, in perils of waters, in perils of robbers, in perils of my own countrymen, in perils of the Gentiles, in perils in the city, in perils in the wilderness, in perils in the sea, in perils among false brethren; in weariness and toil, in sleeplessness often, in hunger and thirst, in fastings often, in cold and nakedness, besides the other things, what comes upon me daily: my deep concern for all the churches."*

Of Saul (prior to being known as Paul), Jesus said of him to Ananias in Acts Chapter 9:15 NKJV: *"Go, for he is a chosen vessel of Mine to bear My name before Gentiles, kings, and the children of Israel. For I will show him how many things he must suffer for my name's sake."* So, as zealous as he once was to persecute people himself, he equally or maybe more so, became zealous for the cause of the Kingdom of God. This is evidenced because *he knew* the persecution he would have to endure, and he still went.

The account of Paul's actual death was not in the bible. There are many theories. The consensus seems to point to the tradition of that time, by being *beheaded*.

CHAPTER THREE

#2- Buildings and Shakings
Received: August 23, 2017

This dream started with me seeing the White House and the Capitol Building, first one, and then the other. I have seen these two buildings many times now. That time, however, was one of the first times.

Each time they were shown to me, I would see them from a distance, and then from very close up. First it was the White House, then the Capitol Building. Each time I saw them close-up, they *shook violently*. Then the scene changed.

I suddenly was in a rural location. I didn't see myself. I simply saw out of my eyes. It was if I was standing in front of large red brick building. It was not the lighter, brighter red or reddish-orange brick, but more of a dark maroon colored brick, like dried blood.

Even within the dream, it seems like there was an importance that I take in every detail of the building itself. So, what seemed like several moments, it was as if I just stood there, just looking, taking it all in.

There was a simplicity to the structure. It was mostly box-like on the front, with little detail really, except the trim on the windows had once been painted a lighter color like white. However, it looked long faded, and with much chipped away over time. There were double doors with something posted like "detail" above the top of the door casing, but it also was only a remnant of what it once was.

You could see one simple filigree-type piece atop the straight part, but you could no longer read what the signage below must've said. It now looked *nondescript* and any special part it had *was now gone.*

Under the double door entry there was a what had been a wide set of white-painted stairs leading in. It looked like they had simply mostly broken apart over time.

I looked up. I saw there were two to three stories. The building was very wide at the face and it was a warm weather season, with bright sunshine. However, my God dreams usually are, even when the content is not good.

I saw that there were tall trees on the same land but positioned left and right along the sides of the building. They appeared to be hundreds of years old. Then the scene changed again.

Now I seemed to be hovering above the front right of the building. It's like I could see down to either the first floor or a basement floor. I saw a woman alone in a dark room. She was wearing pioneer clothing. (Also mentioned in Vol. 3). She was standing in one place or another and often pacing. Then a wall suddenly seemed to start moving in. The same thing seemed to keep happening, always leaving her running toward the front wall or cowering in the corner. At the time, while in the dream, I wondered if she was me and I thought of the saying, "the walls are closing in." However, the Lord *very quickly* shut that line of thought down, and immediately the scene changed. In fact, I *felt* like I'd just been ripped from it!

I found myself very quickly being moved down the right side of the building. I noticed the trees on that side were nowhere in sight now. Just as I was thinking that was odd, we were already at the back right corner, which wasn't that far back. I was looking at a large expanse of land and what was taking place.

In the back there was a man on a backhoe moving back and forth from several piles, sticking the bucket in and then moving to a humongous hole and dumping into it. I seemed to be just there watching for a few moments and then suddenly it was as if I was right up at near the hole. The backhoe came again, and I watched as the bucket dumped. Then I saw, . . . what came from the bucket and what was filling the hole was bodies, just mounds and mounds of dead bodies! Right then I exclaimed, apparently aloud, "What like the Holocaust?" I woke up saying it. It was very unnerving!

Immediately I started asking God all kinds of questions. Right after, still awake, it's like the dream continued but as a vision.

I was standing in front of the building again, and the whole picture view of the building and the surroundings starting to shake, just like the White House and the Capitol Building in the beginning.

Suddenly I was being moved down the left side of the building. I realized that the trees on the left seemed to have moved very far away from the building, almost out of sight. I also noticed that the left side of the building was much deeper than the right. I was paused and made to look up. I realized that now it seemed there were likely four to six stories. At the very end of this part, I could see up behind the entirety of the building. What was highlighted is how the middle rear of the building was not deep at all. The part that would be the back of the right side protruded out some, but seemed oddly *cut short*. Then the back of the left side seemed to go pretty much *the depth of the land.*

Then without a visual on the shift, I was back hovering above the front right of the building and staring down through floors to see the woman in the dark room again. This time, however, she was laying on her side, with her legs slightly bent. She was completely still, or dead. That was the end.

What took me quite a lot of words to explain moved fluidly as I saw it, both sleeping and awake. I knew some of this soon after having it. A large part of the interpretation did not come, though, until I was typing the dream and vision out for this book. Things were being revealed as I was writing, and in a large way, I was surprised at just how plain it seemed in the end. Following is the interpretation.

Interpretation

There will be at least three shakings for the United States, as there were three shakings shown between the dream and vision. It is unclear to date whether they will come *from* Washington D.C. or happen *in* Washington D.C. and then move throughout the country. However, they come, *the U.S. will be shaken.*

The red brick building, which I now have seen many times, showed that death and even mental torture will become commonplace. The woman shown was wearing pioneer clothing, this simply meant those being persecuted will be without modern amenities.

Whether the enormous number of bodies are from before or after the war, or through the persecution of people against people and outside entities coming to govern, is unclear. Though I had thoughts about the pandemic and much fitting the period we have been in for a couple years now, the Lord reminded me He chose this dream and vision for *this* book about **persecution**.

As I was writing this, I believe a new revelation was given. The dimensions of the building has much to do with *left leaning* versus *right leaning*, politically, with the majority of the world by then having a more "left view" which is or will be *the world's view*. Additionally, it is also shown in the differences of the trees, the building's stories and the depths of the right, middle and left. The first view showed everything quite even. The latter views were quite different.

It being shown as a school, is symbolic of the "establishment" in this case, and what will be taught as the acceptable norm' in U.S. society and the world.

The trees, likely hundreds of years old, first stood on each side of the establishment means they stood for that which was regarded as important or what was considered *founding beliefs* and *upright values* by the founding Fathers of that time.

When I saw the trees later, the ones on the right had been removed all together and the ones on the left had been moved so far away that they could barely be seen.

This means that by this point, the right leaning has been removed all together from any authority in lieu of the left leaning, which is then the way of the world and the *world view*. Symbolically, this also showed from the back, with the right side seeming almost cut off.

It also showed that those that were left leaning in that time, will have moved so far from the founding beliefs, that it can barely be seen as the same country it was founded as. Symbolically, this was represented also with the building now being higher, and going as far as the end of the land, or in this case the entirety of the country.

Lastly, the middle portion was barely there. That simply indicates that you will be for the new way, or you will be against it. There will be **no middle ground**.

Lastly, the front of the building was non-descript, except for the front entry. There were two doors and a wide set of steps. I did not see what the little detail was above the doors, but as I started writing this paragraph, I was reminded of Matthew 7:13-14 (NKJV), which says: *"Enter by the narrow gate; for wide is the gate and broad is the way that leads to destruction, and there are many who go in by it. Because narrow is the gate and difficult is the way which leads to life, and there are few who find it."*

Back then, the dream and vision seemed out-of-nowhere. I was almost fixated, taking in all the odd, at the time, details. It was likely so I would remember small pieces all this time later. As dated, it was the end of summer 2017. I've now seen the same school-like structure many times since, so much so it's started feeling familiar to me. Elements of *this* time-period make it seem almost *eerily* familiar. My glimpse was in bright sunshine, but the contents still feel stunningly cold to remember. So, *take heed*.

CHAPTER FOUR

Troubled Waters

When the ministering angels gave me the dreams and visions to be in this book, I was missing information on one and didn't have another at all. I did remember what I'd seen but didn't have much to go on. The original vision was quite a bit before the other parts I was shown recently. That made it hard to remember how it felt then or what thoughts might have flittered through my mind when I had it. Though often much is revealed right away, occasionally, it isn't. Then it becomes an adventure of pressing in, praying, and seeing what is revealed. Thankfully, even though the original vision immediately gave me a feeling, there just really wasn't much to the vision overall.

Though I have mentioned this throughout the book series, I still marvel a bit at the way God gives me the books of this series. All these years I have dreamt, and later started having visions. So much was lost over the years or never noted at all. Yet, poised to write, on each book I always ask what dreams or visions are going to be included, and I am usually given ones that I still have a recording of, notes for, or a memory about, however, fleeting. They are never in the order I received them, and sometimes they have originally been given to me months or even years apart. Despite the things I have seen, it still truly amazes me. With that, let's go on.

#3 -The Taking of America
Received: April 8 – October 23, 2021

Before I relay the 3-part vision, let me just say, I live in the U.S. Despite how some things here no longer seem to be as the country I was born and raised in, I do know I've been quite blessed to live in a country where I've enjoyed freedoms that people in other parts of the world never had. In writing anything like this, I am not attempting to curse America or any other nation. Rather, I am relaying that which I was given and am now directed to share. With that, I prayerfully continue.

Part I
April 8, 2021

This was a short vision. Simply, I saw a handful of small boats with motors, not far from the beach my view seemed to come from. It was if I was standing on the shore. Men were standing in the water. They were not far out, as the water seemed about waist high on most of them. The feeling I had at the time was one of dread. Without words, I knew that these men had arrived *undetected* and with bad intent.

Part II
October 23, 2021- #1

I saw one man standing in the water, a little less than waist high. The same kind of small boat with motor I saw before was a little behind him. Then I was made to look again. My view seemed to be from further right and then was *made to look* down. I saw two torpedoes lying beside each other, where the beach meets the water. I then looked up and saw the man standing on the beach with an assault rifle. He seemed posed, or in a *military stance*. Yet, *I knew* he was not "ours". (meaning, not "American")

Part III
October 23, 2021- #2

I saw what looked like a package being put into what appeared a tuba-shaped pipe atop a military ship. I did not see who was putting it in, rather it appeared as I just saw the package being moved into the opening, as if by invisible hands.

Interpretation

The initial vision was simply showing that men will invade the United States shoreline undetected. They will have ill intent.

The second part was simply continuing the scene but at a closer view. That is why I only saw one man and one boat.

My view changed from looking straight at him, to me seeing from a position to the right, where I then saw the two torpedoes. The coast will take two hits, and then the men will invade a little north of the pummeling.

When I looked again and saw the man with the assault rifle, standing in a military pose, it simply means that the U.S. will be invaded by outside military or military-type forces.

The third part was the military ship. After having the second part of the vision, the torpedoes, I'd ask the Lord how it happened. That's when I saw this part.

So, though it was seen last, it takes place first. The military ship takes a hit, which was shown as receiving a package. The part that was shown receiving the package was tuba shaped. The tuba, a musical instrument, would seem to be plugged by the package, I feel it will come without warning and they will not be able to sound any alarm. (End of original interpretation)

I was not given anything that told me that this was the U.S. east coast in the visions, but *I knew* that it was. I made a couple notations when writing down what dreams or visions would be in this book. When I noted this one, all I had was "dream about bad men reaching the eastern shores without being detected" and later, "detonates a bomb that levels a city in South Carolina".

Today, writing this, I was talking to the Lord about a vision called "Scene on a Beach," which is already published in Take Heed- The Elijah Anointing-Vol. 3". It seemed to possibly be the approximate area that the vision parts in this chapter are. In it, an IED detonated somewhere in proximity to a beach. Also in it, I was also flown southeast prior to the rest of what I saw. I live in Ohio, so I knew it was the east coast!

Naturally, today I was asking if this event was another part of that, or if it is separate. The answer seems to be that these events are connected, or the events are part of a *connected timeline*.

Continuing to pray that day, I saw "WAR after treaty fails". That obviously added a new dimension to this. So, it has been days until now, being able to get back to it. I continued to pray since then, asking for answers to be able to correctly explain what I've seen, and my continued in-terpretation follows.

As in "Scene on a Beach," in Vol. 3, a bomb is detonated somewhere in South Carolina near a beach, and it levels a city. This is *internal*. The ministering angels revealed that two nations sent terrorists into the U.S. They are or will be already here. It was inferred that they set off this bomb. What was portrayed in Vol. 3 was the aftermath of *that* action.

At some point later, the WAR happens after a failed treaty. The scenes relayed in this chapter are of a ship being bombed, the east coast being torpedoed, and men invading the coast. *I knew* this happens in South Carolina, and in prayer since I have been given that the visions for this chapter affect both S.E. South Carolina and N.E. Georgia.

Lastly, I felt that after a dirty bomb detonates in South Carolina (Vol. 3), that the area becomes seen dramatically weakened, and so in war, (Vol. 4), it becomes a target.

#4 -A Titanic Takeover

The back-story on this one is that quite some time ago I was given just a small part of what was to be this portion. I wrote it down and then nothing more was told about it. Now having done all the book but this part and the last part of the last chapter, He brought me back to it.

Received: Unknown Date

The ministering angel started speaking to me about two countries. He said a man would visit the ship, under the *guise* of something, but really having bad intent. The feeling at the time was that it was one of the leaders of one of the countries, either *political* or *governmental*. I knew that the ship would sink, and the real reason was because one of the two countries wanted control of the shipping lanes. I was never given who or how it was sank.

Received: February 8, 2022

This came in pieces throughout the day and night. It should be noted, I saw some of it, and other parts were either relayed or literally spelled out.

Part 1: I saw water and a beach. The scene panned out a bit and I could see a larger view of what looked like an ocean kind-of bumping the beach area. It was not violently bumping, just bumping. Then it was as if I saw water suddenly rescinding from the beach quickly, and a big wave forming.

Part 2: (This part was relayed) "A wall is ravaged by U.N. troops. It ignites a U.N. divide." "A military ship that sank is left stretching across the Thames."

Part 3: The burial on the Thames. This is a latter-day Titanic. It is a huge ship with many people lost.

Part 4: I saw a tent first, it panned out and then I saw men lying in sleeping bags next to each other in rows on both sides of a curved outdoor walkway. Then I saw the words: "The Eiffel Tower becomes a refuge for men of war."

Part 5: The President of France wants to close a train that runs through England and France. Then the French government talks at the U.N. It is deemed that the water ways are too blocked to shut down the train; and *France is undone.* They leave with a warning that England *better try* to move the ship at Thames!

It will result in *guile.* England was already waiting for the wall to collapse. England is ready to take over control of all the shipping channels.

Part 6: Then France decides to "store" the train; however, the train comes full of U.N. military, and England takes over France.

CHAPTER FIVE

When the Fight Comes Home

Before I start the dream and vision, I just want to relay a few things about them. They were very puzzling to me, a little scary as well, and I came away with many questions which were not immediately answered. In fact, at least one still has not been answered.

Though I had regularly posted on a social media channel then, I did not post this right away. Then when I did, I did not describe at least half the details, still not sure why I saw all I'd seen. I did have notes but did not relay them. I thought I eventually recorded what I had later but have been unable to find it. With that, let's go on.

#5 Not Fair 8 15, 26 x 42 or 26 – 42
Received: Dream – August 15, 2017

I woke up, in conversation with the Lord or a ministering angel and said aloud, "That's not fair." Then I heard "As you say, life is not always fair." Then I said, "Well let me reiterate, life is not fair, and we should not hope that it is fair, because if it was fair, then we'd all get what we deserve, but Jesus paid the cost for us." Then I kept asking what was not fair in the dream, and I heard either "twenty-six by forty-two" or "twenty-six to forty-two."

Received: Vision – August 15, 2017 (upon waking)

I woke up asking, "What's not fair?" Then, I had a vision. It started as if I was entering the tall side of my husband's building. It is 18-20 ft. high. It was as if I was seeing out of my eyes and entered in about half-way. I looked to my right, seemingly just in time, to see a large elephant passing on the far right, closely followed by a giraffe. Almost simultaneously, I saw an aquatic tank passing by in mid-air. I first saw a dolphin, then an octopus with its tenacles moving in all directions. At that point, I looked back to the right and saw a large brown bear. It was simply standing, but wearing a vest and a fez and watching it all.

Then I looked left, and huge beings were walking or gliding into the building. They were very tall, much taller than me, and their body size fit their height. They appeared as two males in long robed attire walking straight in, a pirate with fancy period clothing who entered talking and laughing toward one that looked like a Jewish Rabbi. The one that looked like a Rabbi had long curls, a hat, and was dressed in black.

I heard nothing but was *made to look* up to the loft that is in that part of my husband's building, and he was there. He, and several others were up in the loft.

The way it was built, there is a long horizontal piece that is see-through, to let sunlight into that building. It was open, like it had been taken out, and he and the others with him had rifles and were shooting toward the southwest, which is where our house sits. Basically, they were furiously moving and shooting from the window right toward the house! Though I could not hear, it was continuous, frantic action, and *I knew* they were both giving fire and getting fired upon.

After the vision, I had more questions. I wondered if it was literal or symbolic. I asked who was there with him, and why he was there. I also wanted to know who was shooting at them from the direction of our house. I asked about timelines and details of the all the pieces and parts that seemed almost like a circus that took a dramatic turn. Following is the interpretation I was given, including one small but seemingly important piece that was given just this morning.

Interpretation
Received: Various Dates

By this time, the U.S. has already been invaded by military-type forces and mercenaries from other countries.

Mercenaries from Africa will be hired to collect and/or kill people that are resisting. They were represented by the *elephant* and the *giraffe*. Today, I was given at least two areas they will come from: Tanzania and Botswana. Currently, I do not know if mercenaries will come from other places too.

A level above the mercenaries, will be *military-type* people from both Japan and China. These were shown as the *dolphin*, representing Japan, and China, represented by the *Octopus*. Japan will have a lessor role or will be directed by China. Additionally, China will have many parts in what is taking place at that time. It will be basically, second in command, answering only to the *bear*, which is Russia. China will be a force on the ground along with others, but the feeling was they also would have a part with technology or *technological weapons.*

Russia, the bear, may not initially seem to be involved, but is "standing back", watching and overseeing the entirety of the operations. However, it will be clear who is in charge when these events start happening. It is also clear at this point, people are still resisting.

Skipping ahead to the gunfight, the fight will come right to people's front doors. In this case, my husband and others took cover in the building, meaning the mercenaries already had the house. They were furiously moving and shooting, re-loading, etc., but the enemy kept firing.

To end the interpretation, I was told the two beings who walked in silently were angels. The pirate in the fancy fitted period clothing represented the devil or one that came for the devil, and the one that looked like a Jewish Rabbi was also an angel.

Basically, they were there because my husband and the others shown represented people who will resist what will take place, many of which will die. The tall beings shown *came to collect their own.*

Apparently, there were believers there, with at least one of them a Messianic Jew. Today I was told that is why one looked like a Rabbi. The two angels who came in first and the angel that looked like a Rabbi were collecting the believers as they died.

At least one man, was also resisting what was happening, just as the others, but had not accepted Christ. The demonic angel pirate was collecting him. An added note here is that I tend to think that there were likely more believers and unbelievers present in the loft, being collected as they passed. One, there were two angels in first, then the others. Also, when I looked up at the flurry, I know there was quite a few more than four men.

I knew when I had the vision, and it was amplified when I was given the overall interpretation, that there will be those that will strongly resist not just the way the world has gone, but the factions who have invaded and have taken over. Though not all that resist will not be caught, imprisoned, or killed, *most will be*. The weaponry and arsenal they will be up against, will be *astoundingly huge*.

This afternoon when I was asking about the specifics, I was shown the angels moving with baskets in their hands. As one flew by me, I saw many dead, lying side by side in neat rows, as if tucked in the basket with great care. It was as if the angel flew by in slow-motion, making sure I could see what their mission had been, and how many were dying.

I saved the beginning for the end. The title I chose was something I heard when I first asked what the dream was, before I had the vision. I had heard either "26 x 42," or "26-42." During the midst I knew it was **"26-42"** *months*, and that what happened in the vision, happens in the Tribulation. Therefore, more pointedly, the things I saw in the vision will occur during months 26–42.

As I was finishing writing the end of the interpretation, thoughts started flittering through my mind. They ended up leading me to Romans 8:25-37 NKJV, which says: *"Who shall separate us from the love of Christ? Shall tribulation, or distress, or persecution, or famine, or nakedness, or peril, or sword? As it is written: "For Your sake we are killed all day long; We are accounted as sheep for the slaughter." Yet in all these things we are more than conquerors through Him who loved us."*

The humanness in me always feels a hedging when I am asked to present something like this. I get no enjoyment out of relaying hard things. I am also not cursing any people or any country. I am simply relaying that which I have been shown and instructed to tell, period.

Honestly, even though I am not well known, I have taken a lot of flak from people I know, and don't know, *in my own* country. So please know this about me. I feel truly blessed to have been born in a country where I have gotten to enjoy many freedoms that so many around the world have never been afforded

The God equation is the one thing that usurps the pride or love of country though. God is holy. He gave man and woman free will. He will not interfere with it or that would make Him a liar, and Numbers 23:19 says: "*God is not a man, that He should lie, Nor a son of man, that He should repent. Has He said, and will He not do? Or has He spoken, and will He not make it good?*" NKJV.

Plus, if you believe, you should know the end of the book. Unfortunately, most believers do not believe that we are heading toward the end. Most believers side with the world that feels people have cried out "The end is near!" for hundreds, even thousands of years. Many either do not know the end of the Book at all, or they refuse to see it is currently playing out before them. For those that do know, *we cannot stay silent.* If we truly love those around us, as we should, our hearts should break for those that do not know Him. For nothing here holds hope. *He* is their hope.

CHAPTER SIX

Persecution Now & Coming

It isn't that we have not witnessed at least some religious persecution in the United States. Certainly, we have. We have also witnessed people being persecuted for any number of warped reasons here and around the world.

As a believer in Christ, yes, maybe we have experienced light-hearted or even hateful jokes, some ostracization, or some other verbal assault, just because we believe. On several occasions people have also been shot in churches and had their churches burned down. Perhaps some have even experienced far worse.

Still, persecution in this country due to believing in or following Jesus Christ does not remotely compare with what believers in Jesus Christ around the globe have experienced.

This country, originally founded with Christian ideals, has given believers born here or those who have come here, so much freedom to know Him and follow Him with little to no fear of anything at all happening to them. Many Christians in countries all around the world have never had that benefit. So, I want to say boldly, again, and without shame, people who have been born in or have come to the United States that are Christian, or even are not, *have been blessed*. Until you understand the gravity of what others have done or fought or died for, you cannot fully appreciate what you have been given *freely*. I hope before this book's end, you consider what, so far, you have escaped. We, here, should all be grateful and *take heed*.

To go on, I could take two to three long paragraphs just naming countries where, **right now**, persecution is happening to people that believe and have relationship with Jesus.

There is extortion, kidnappings, mutilations, imprisonments, slavery, having basic rights taken away, being forced to live scavenging for food or water, even in thriving places. In some places, to have a bible means death, yet people still delight to *die* just to get one! Then, of course, there are places where many people have or still can die *just because they believe*.

Two occasions of persecution from recent years immediately enter my mind. Both happened in places we don't normally "think" of Christians. Maybe my connections to these places make me recall these more quickly than others. Certainly, they aren't the only horrible things that have happened or are still happening.

I had ties to Libya through a Libyan friend and his family I acquired through business. That business then brought three others to me that I came to know and respect. Suddenly I knew people living in Egypt, Libya, Tunisia, and Turkey, and knew people from and in Pakistan as well.

As far as Pakistan, I had met and had business association with many from Pakistan. Additionally, the church I was in for many years had cultivated relationships with many completely "sold-out-for-Jesus" Christians. Many times, the Pastor, his wife, and a handful of others would physically go there to assist the growing sister-church, putting themselves in peril of all the same dangers the Pakastani Christians were experiencing, and still are.

In 2016, in Lahore, Pakistan, seventy-two men, women and children were killed while they worshipped in an Easter celebration in a park, by a suicide bomb. An offshoot group of the Pakastani Taliban took responsibility. As Muslim is the recognized religion, the Christians worshipping God and doing it in a public park was an affront to those responsible. After, that pastor requested prayer, but he and the people remained faithful, despite *great* and *crushing loss*.

In December of 2014 and January of 2015, a total of twenty Egyptians and one Ghanaian, all contractors, were kidnapped by ISIL in Libya. They were Coptic Christians. In February a video came out on social media and news stations from somewhere in Iraq. It showed the contractors, then dressed in orange jumpsuits, made to kneel in the sand of a beach in Sirte, Libya. They had refused to refute their belief. To be honest, I'm not sure it would have mattered. With camera rolling they were beheaded for all the world to see.

In both cases, whether they had counted the cost before or not, they had to have counted it then. When faced with the devastating circumstances . . . and death, they chose *life* in Him.

Jesus Christ

He was both hailed and mocked. He was sought out for miracles and to be taken captive. He'd been belittled and abandoned by His own, even betrayed by some of the ones closest to Him.

His ministry time didn't start until He was about thirty. He was hated by the religious leaders because they could not seem to stop Him, but also could not really refute Him or the miracles that happened through Him at the same time. The way they had presented or handled belief and the people, was not His way. In fact, He said, *"Woe to you, teachers of the law and Pharisees, you hypocrites! You travel over land and sea to win a single convert, and when you have succeeded, you make them twice as much a child of hell as you are."* Matt. 23:15-33 NIV.

On the way to ultimate death on earth, He was left to die, and a murderer was granted freedom instead, by crowds of the same people He had come to save. As if that wasn't terrible enough, He was scourged with a whip that likely had iron balls and sharpened bones of sheep or some other animal. His skin wasn't just cut, it literally would have been torn away with every one of the lashes that hit him. Even though most scholars assume it would have been thirty-nine lashes, because that was a Jewish tradition, the scourging was by the Roman soldiers. Still, He was beaten beyond recognition and bleeding profusely, close to ending His life. Then He was made to carry a wooden cross to the place of the skull, "Golgotha." However, He was so badly injured that partway there, a soldier ordered a man in the crowd to carry His cross the rest of the way. Then they nailed Him to it, with a sign that roughly translates as, "This is Jesus, King of the Jews," and they hung Him up for all to see with a crown of thorns pushed down around his head, causing more pain and suffering.

They placed Him between two thieves, one of which mocked Him as some of the crowd. Despite everything,

He basically pardoned the second thief, who verbally stood up for Him, stating they deserved what they got, but He did nothing that deserved death. Jesus promised him that they would be together that day, in Paradise.

As his mom and a few friends stood by watching the heart-wrenching event, soldiers cast lots for his clothing. Still, even in His agony, He asked the Father, "Forgive them, for they know not what they do," found in Luke 23:34 KJV. So, to end this portion, take heed what Jesus said about persecution.

"If the world hates you, you know that it hated Me before it hated you. If you were of the world, the world would love its own. Yet because you are not of the world, but I chose you out of the world, therefore the world hates you. Remember the word that I said to you, 'A servant is not greater than his master.' If they persecuted Me, they will also persecute you.' But all these things they will do to you for My name's sake, because they do not know Him who sent Me." John 15:18-21 NKJV

#6 -A Dark World with an AI Savior
Received: 1/11/2022

When I was given this title awhile back, I was shocked. I called my friend Marcia because I just needed to say it to someone. However, I didn't even call her right away. I think it was a couple of days later. Maybe despite all that I have seen or been told, it seemed to still take me aback a bit. Yet, it also didn't. Maybe the time I mulled it over a bit before telling her, was simply me trying to make peace with it myself.

At the same time there were parts of me then, and now, that thought it made perfect sense. Although, much of that came from remembering that many times in the last years while reading the word, or thinking about things I saw changing in the world, a thought about an *AI entity* and the *"beast system"* popped into my head. I never allowed myself to entertain it, thinking it was my imagination or a demon trying to take me off track. I would always remind myself that the word said, *"Here is wisdom. Let him who has understanding calculate the number of the beast, for it is the number of a man: His number is 666,"* Revelation 13:18 However, I also never took it to God, 'til now.

Received: 2/12/2022

The first thing I was told was at the time of Tribulation, this book would be banned. I am not sure if that happens before or at that time. Then, the ministering angels continued.

A *DAS STE* makes a world where people live taking pills that return them to health, and money is not needed. A man talks to the people as they immerse themselves in the virtual world that takes them anywhere they want to go.

An A.I., predicts war, and that "practice-time" is over. It then tells them that if they take *the mark*, they will not have to take the *antidote pill* any more. So, most everyone wants to take the mark, which is an *all A.I.- directed program*.

At first, the man and the A.I. directed program seem like the answer to all the world's problems, but it is short-lived. The *unsaid*, the *real directive* of the plan is to take over humanity.

During this period, the man rises to world stature, as

does his "prophet", the A.I. He talks to everyone and ingratiates himself everywhere for a time. However, he also takes the starving to test the biotechnology, but they love him because they are fed, housed, and want for nothing. Unfortunately, later he alters the tech so they will kill anyone who refuses the mark, because by then it is mandatory.

This man is the Antichrist spoken about in the Bible toward the end of Revelation 13. The A.I. that predicts things that then happen, is the man's prophet, which also *causes* things to happen in the natural realm and to people, making the man appear to do miraculous things. People will believe all sorts of things: that he is Jesus returned, that he's a God, that he is God, etc. His fan base will be worldwide.

Ultimately though, this man and this ever-advancing technology will cause many who have *not been deceived* to be put to *death*. Christians will be hated and sought, as well as other dissenters.

In the end, he will speak boldly and opening, blaspheming God and Jesus Christ, and stand in the re-built temple in Israel, proclaiming that he, and he alone, *is GOD.*

We need to address the spiritual piece of this. The man might be a man that operates with extremely advanced technology, but the man, himself, has given himself over to *satan*, who is diabolically opposed to the true and living God. This is the same satan that was Lucifer, a beautiful angel in heaven, that God created. He had high authority. However, he exalted himself above God, and basically tried a take-over. He was cast out, along with 1/3 of the angels, who chose him over GOD. Therefore, please understand *where* the man's power *truly* comes from.

Lastly, God has not hidden Himself from this world, even creation shows his existence. Proverbs 14:12 NKJV says: *"There is a way that seems right to a man, but its end is the way of death."* Hear me, if you are here when all this happens, *do not take the mark*! If you do, you no longer have ability to come to God at all! *He has given us all free will to choose* to do things, believe, seek Him, and come to Him, *or not*.

Those who choose the way the world goes, will ultimately be choosing *satan* over *God*. They will be choosing hell over heaven, and that choice is *eternal*.

The Word in Revelation 14: 9-10 says: *"And another angel, a third, followed them, saying with a loud voice, "If anyone worships the beast and its image and receives a mark on his forehead or on his hand, he also will drink the wine of God's wrath, poured full strength into the cup of his anger, and he will be tormented with fire and sulfur in the presence of the holy angels and in the presence of the Lamb."*

So, please *take heed!*

ABOOKS

ALIVE Book Publishing and ALIVE Publishing Group
are imprints of Advanced Publishing LLC,
3200 A Danville Blvd., Suite 204, Alamo, California 94507

Telephone: 925.837.7303
alivebookpublishing.com

www.ingramcontent.com/pod-product-compliance
Lightning Source LLC
LaVergne TN
LVHW041209080426
835508LV00008B/872